NOWHERE SPECIAL

LINDA FRANCE *writes:*

Nowhere Special is something special – poetry that combines anger and affirmation, Englishness and the European, the shock of the new and banners of tradition, rhetoric and urban lyricism, 'grief and beauty spinning round and round'.

The collection's driving force is a disappointed desire 'to live without regret'. However Andy Croft's unfailing generosity and faith in the achievements of people against the odds maps out 'this lovely world', transforming his nowhere into an everywhere 'as it never was but still might be'.

Croft's fearlessness in broaching History and Political Idealism is finely tuned to his uncompromising sonorous tones and range of steely rhythms. If a 'whole world needs unbreaking', *Nowhere Special* is a good enough place to start.

For Nikki

NOWHERE SPECIAL

Andy Croft

Andy C.

FLAMBARD

ACKNOWLEDGEMENTS

Some of these poems have appeared in the following publications:
An Abacus of Bats, Breathless, The Brecht Year Book,
Critical Survey, The Evening Gazette, A Hole Like That,
Iron, Leaving for Cape Horn, The New Statesman,
The Northern Echo, Northern Electric News, Red Herring,
Scratch, Teesside Writers Workshop 3,
Tees Valley Writer, Verses United, Writearound the Year.

The following poems carry specific dedications:
'Nineteen Ninety-One' – Hanna Behrend; 'Rathaus' – Bill Herbert;
'Forbidden Fruit' – Ken Worpole; 'New Times' – Andrea Ehrit-Kinsky;
'Rounton Grange' – Malcolm Chase; 'Come On You Reds' – Mark Robinson;
'Wake' – Cynthia and Dave Goldstein; 'Redcar Sands' – Barbara Gamble;
'My Favourite Martian' – Martin Szebeni; 'Leaving for Cape Horn' –
Peter Challoner; 'Living and Learning' – Rebecca O'Rourke;
'Mahler's Fifth' – Mike Wilson; 'Beadnell Bay' – Jack, Joe and Alick.

I wish to thank Northern Arts for an Award in 1994
which bought valuable time to work on these poems.
A. C.

Cover and author photographs by Dermot Blackburn.
Cover design by Mike Davis.

Flambard Press wishes to thank Northern Arts for its financial support.

Published in 1996 by Flambard Press
4 Mitchell Avenue, Jesmond, Newcastle upon Tyne, NE2 3LA

Typeset by Pandon Press Ltd, Newcastle upon Tyne
in association with Mary Holcroft Veitch
Printed by Cromwell Press, Broughton Gifford, Melksham, Wiltshire

A CIP catalogue record for this book is available from the British Library
ISBN 1 873226 22 5
© Andy Croft

CONTENTS

And where do all these sodden trunks
come from, thousands and thousands of them drifting by,
utterly empty and abandoned to the waves? I wail and I swim.
Business, I wail, as usual, everything lurching, everything
under control, everything OK, my fellow beings probably drowned
in the drizzle, a pity, never mind, I bewail them, so what?
Dimly, hard to say why, I continue to wail, and to swim.
                           (Hans Magnus Enzensberger)

For what does it matter if it rains all day?
And what's the good of knowing
Which way the wind is blowing
When whichever way it blows it's a cold rain now?
                           (Norman Nicholson)

It's all my fault. I must have done somebody wrong.
                           (Elmore James)

NINETEEN NINETY-ONE

It was a bright, warm day in August
And the clocks were striking midnight.
Trailing dreams like rags behind her,
She fell down the steps from the light
Of the Winter Palace, stumbling on pumpkins,
Ensnared with dead flowers, feeling the bite
Of the rats.

The youngest child, the favoured one,
Sleeps tonight on the streets. It's cold,
Selling matchsticks under bright stars,
Fairy tales of abuse, junk, bought-and-sold,
Waste, extermination. Someone's been telling lies,
The new world order meets the old,
Among the rats.

The weak, the speechless, the sometimes good,
Can depend on this – the cold hearth, the bad,
The vile wind, the dreams of dancing,
Their own limitless patience, an earth so sad
And ourselves the perfect fit,
The best luck the enemy ever had.
And the rats.

RATHAUS

Ring out the bells, the cat is dead!
The ancient, toothless, useless, sight-
less, sleepy, flea-bag, carnivore
Whose reign of terrifying claws
Kept rats from sleeping in their beds
With dreams of hot-breathed laws –
Is put to sleep without a fight.

Old *Koschka*'s fallen down the well –
Rejoice! Tuck in! The farm is yours!
Let starveling democrats get fat
While there's no cat to smell a rat.
All those who dared not hang a bell
Around the neck of comrade cat
Can dine tonight on the applause

Of all the little rat-faced men
Whose long-tailed, sharp-eyed hunger gnaws
Their guts with dreams of meat, can toast
To killing paper tigers, boast
Of how the *kolkhoz* yard again
Belongs to those who have a nose
For shedding blood in Freedom's cause.

For once they know the cat is dead
The smallest farmyard creatures should
Not grow surprised if rats grow fat.
Or if these portly democrats
Who feed on appetites more red
In tooth and claw than any cat
Are drawn to midnight smells of blood.

So Parliament is stormed by tanks
To ratify their sharp-toothed State.
A terrifying paradise
Of sewer rats and harvest mice.
And so a grateful world gives thanks
And hunger starts to rise in price
And Freedom starts to put on weight.

And who will pipe this plague away?
And who will pipe this plague away?

FORBIDDEN FRUIT

'Behind our house was the end of a small garden
which was full of fruit trees where now and again
we scrumped apples.' (Erich Honecker)

The sound of teasing apples' soft, wet fall
On someone else's orchard floor is harder
Still when bread and turnip-syrup's all
You've had for breakfast, dinner, tea, the larder

Empty as a child who knows the laws
Of property and hunger off by heart.
But hunger is an honourable cause
As scrumping apples is an ancient art,

And every child must one day learn to choose
Between what's right and wrong, and pay the price
Of wanting something more than bread, and lose
The childish appetite for Paradise.

If what you are is what you eat, the taste
Of fruit you never knew's the life you could
Have shared; and hungry children never waste
The chance to eat sweet things they know aren't good

For them. And walls are meant to keep out these
Who live on bread and turnips, though they know
It's always greener somewhere else, like trees
In walled and private orchards where they grow

That wormy, soft, sweet fruit which nourishes
The knowledge that, though every apple fall,
Another Paradise still flourishes
As always, just beyond another wall.

THE PATHS OF RIGHTEOUSNESS

In memory of Jim Atkinson

Even geology must shove when pushed, when glaciers say,
And hills like dry-stone walls come tumbling down; the best,
Most splendid, roaring volcanoes all exhaust their fires one day
And woolly ideologies must all be fleeced like sheep.

The world was all before them, where to choose their place of rest.
And Providence their guide; expropriate, these sheep now sleep
Where shepherds slept and bandits dined, musicians on their way
To Bremen town, munching the commons, a sit-down protest,

A collective farm. Wading waist-high through nettles that day
In August, we disturbed them grazing, watched them queue to leap
Through broken windows. But some old rams, bigger than the rest,
Upstairs, couldn't face the steps down, sat bleating on a heap

Of their own shit, 'State of Emergency'. All they possessed
Were ruins, and with the other sheep we climbed the path's steep
And wandering steps and slow through Eden took our solitary way.

THE WORKS OF GIANTS

Splendid this rampart, though fate destroyed it.
Strange was its building, but fall was strangest.
Mighty the giants who must have made it.
Bitter the wind that blows through ruins,
Coldest the moon that hoops its shadows
Dark through rubble of best ambition,
Dark through the halls where rats are creeping
Over the faces of stone-dead builders.
Bitter the day when walls fell earthwards
Coldest the day that broke on ruin.
Long was the building, short the falling,
Gone are the builders, never returning.

NEW TIMES

I sit in a flat tonight on the Tierpark,
Excited and afraid, watching half a world catch light
On the edge of this last decade.

Today's democratic rain fell impartially,
A late and lovely Spring in a city of goods trains,
Tramlines, bus stops. The public thing

The public thing denied so long's alive on
The overhead railway, on the underground, the wide
Crowds moving on Karl-Marx-Allee.

Imagine a young town with a rebuilt past,
New flats already old, waiting for a future gone
Away, inside, out of the cold.

Barbarians are recalled everywhere, the past
Besieges this enclosed place, a private city, walled,
Looking History in the face –

Walk along Artur-Becker-Straße, take a tram ride
To the Ernst Thaelmann Park, past Dimitroff. The flicker-
ing lights of pain blink in the dark.

Built with yesterday's rubble, designed for earth, this
Humane metropolis's blue skies prove vulnerable
As the Athenian Polis.

O City of God, with your lakes, gardens and fountains,
Republic of Good, St Augustine's promise breaks,
As the Elect always knew that it would

And Pelagian heresies flower in parks
While a late fall of snow on Liebknecht-Straße pleases
Upturned faces. Nature is slow

And surprising, forests green with knowledge in leaf
Where happiness is still resisted by her children
Enjoying their fortunate fall.

Night past, the wet morning breaks on deserted streets
Glistening with liberties. We make our own mistakes
In our own time, but not as we please.

And so shall the world go on. Trees blown down at night
Roll like statues, headless, on a windswept horizon,
A new earth, an age of endless

Date. Though the future we must live in's no longer
Ours just for the taking, there's still friendship's work and trust.
A whole world still needs unbreaking.

NO PLACE LIKE HOME

'I cannot well perceive (the world being as it is, and so
many poor people therein) how any man be rich and
keep rich without damnation therefore.' (Thomas More)

OK, I lied, I made it up. I never saw no place
Nowhere the like of it. That old moneyless
Res publica, the dream of common wealth, of decent folk,
Was just a fiction, just a scream, a private, Latin joke.
All that stuff – full employment, six-hour day,
The public hospitals, communal kitchens every evening,
Even the toilets made of gold – no chance, no way.

Good lies all the same, worth the telling and the listening.

I never saw the like of it, but still I wish I had.
Some comfort agaynst trybulacion and such bad,
Against dissolution everywhere, against harm, progress.
Just another satire sponsored by the Congress
For Cultural Freedom, the builders of heaven on earth
Raising hell. There's no place like a market place for selling,
It's true, for slaves in gold chains to find their worth.

Bad truths all the same, worth the listening and the telling.

AFTER THE SINKING OF THE TITANIC

The rain holds up the falling clouds,
The mountain-sea withstands the rain,
Here History quickly turns to ice,
And iceberg ranges take the strain.
We sink and swim and sing as best we can,

Adrift upon this bitter night,
And wait for dawn at last to break
Upon the land of lost content,
And hope next time we won't mistake
It for the sleeping, cold Leviathan

That swallowed whole the world's last hope
In sight of palm-fringed paradise.
One day perhaps the moon might thaw.
Till then we drift upon the ice
Like human hearts held fast in iceberg frost.

My hopes are gone and stars still fall
And still the dragon's horrid tail
Threatens our little ship of fools,
And in the belly of the whale
Are good designs still with their authors lost.

GETTING NOWHERE

'The state and happiness of these poor people was thus, in
a dream or vision, represented to me. I saw, as if they were
set on the sunny side of a mountain, there refreshing
themselves with the pleasant beams of the sun, while I was
shivering and shrinking in the cold...' (John Bunyan)

Far out to sea, far west of Spain and far from home
Lies the land men call Cokaygne, where love still rides
In crystal cloisters deep beneath the sea
That yet may catch the sunlight on the foam
As icecaps melt, oceans swell and boisterous tides
Wash golden mountain peaks like accidie.

Where once they dreamed of mountains in the sunlight,
Swimming naked in cold baptismal streams
Where History would begin its final course
And engulf one day the cities of the night,
Now I wake still tired from hot and thirsty dreams,
From climbing dry riverbeds back to their source,

Or from cold, green, underwater, nightmare wrecks
Drifting like icebergs, unfinished stories,
Broken hulks and promises, washed up, left high and dry,
Chained like Prometheus and the Bolsheviks,
Between two worlds, the mirror and the glories.
We'll walk those green pastures by and by, by and by.

Before the Flood they dreamed of human riches,
Where all should shine and spangle among the fountains,
But all hope's damned from Milton to Stalin. Waters rise,
Heads down, we're now too busy mending ditches
To recall Prometheus in the mountains,
Whole again, watching the dawn with open eyes.

NOWHERE SPECIAL

*'Men fight and lose the battle, and the thing that they fought
for comes about in spite of their defeat, and when it comes turns
out not to be what they meant, and other men have to fight
for what they meant under another name.'* (William Morris)

Please don't mind us, we're doing just fine –
You keep your endless night, that night where we
Beneath the stained-glass stars laid schemes
For England as it never was but still might be,
Those lovely, childhood paintbox fields of dreams.
You keep your future, I'll keep mine.
Your thousand, thousand, thousand hungry all their lives
Utopians no doubt who want what they can't get,
And get what they don't want, a world where none survives
The scrutiny of money, markets, interest, debt.

For History happens somewhere, never gets nowhere,
And dreaming art makes futures come unstuck,
So foolish hedge priests glimpse through thorns the stars
And trace illuminated heavens in a book
They cannot read; and so through prison bars
In Bedford or St Petersburg, somehow, somewhere,
The dreaming cities of the future glitter still.
And who can judge them, who can tell
How long that night remained a fortress, why they built
Not cities but a barracks, woke inside another cell?

But if one day you pick the lock of your own powers,
And if the flood beyond the walls at last subsides,
Revealing dreams of fields where lie unblessed
All those who drowned when History burst its sides,
Who tried to drain the anger of the dispossessed,
Who sowed their hope in all the soil they knew – there flowers
Still that ancient future, underwater, out of season,
Where, as in a dream, we slowly swim through this dark night
Till waves shall break at last on human reason
And we wake blinking in the day's new light.

ROUNTON GRANGE

'He heard Morris talking and walking about in
an excited way, and went to inquire if anything
was wrong. "He turned on me like a wild animal –
'It is only that I spend my life in ministering to
the swinish luxury of the rich.'"'
(W.R. Lethaby, *William Morris as Work-Master*,
about Sir Lowthian Bell, Teesside iron-master)

It's more than forty years ago
Since nowhere never was,
And nothing's changed, except we know
That nothing can, because

Another bloody century's passed
Since nowhere might have been,
And nowhere changes like the past,
And somewhere in between

Imagination and despair,
The history of dreams,
The future's somehow lost, somewhere,
And nowhere's what it seems.

Here every anger turns to seed
And beauty back to dirt,
And money changes back to greed
And hope to dust: like art

Which, living in one world in fact,
Another in desire,
Showed poor England what it lacked,
And what it still requires.

The thoroughness of that dissent!
Hired by uncommon wealth,
By Iron Masters, who, content
That others lived in filth,

Bought swinish luxury and pride
To hide what they had done
And found they'd bought an art which tried
To show how freedom's won!

But nothing lasts and nothing's left,
And hope, like art, soon dies,
Like long dead patterns' ghostly breath
Traced on the walls of sties

Long since pulled down. (Unlike the class
Who watched while others built,
Who hoped that art might yet outlast
The dirt they hid with gilt,

Who owned the useless toil that turned
Their money into art
And back again, a trick first learned
By making cash from dirt

In towns like this.) Still dirt endures
Though useless toil's long gone,
Its uselessness as useless for
The class that sat upon

The profit others' toil once earned,
As toil was ever profitless
For those who builded here and learned
To live in ugliness.

A kind of justice this – that walls
Once built for men to sit
In swinish luxury should all
Be ruins when those not fit

For pigs survive! As art decays
When rich men's houses crumble,
So, at last, one famous day
All Property shall tumble

Down, when all shall share, possess
The thing we've always known:
That nowhere won't be built unless
By those who nowhere own.

COME ON YOU REDS

The winter tilts towards late afternoon
As the pitch soaks up the first rain, the last light.
Standing up here in the Holgate End,

Good humoured, bad tempered and always right,
Self-mockery keeps the cold out. A cartoon
Working class that forgot how to defend

And never knew how to attack. So many
Defeats. But still the floodlights gild the pitch
With flame, and something's still at stake:

A consciousness of sorts – but which?
A glorious, phosphorous epiphany
(It's Stuart Ripley on the break!)

It's the triumph of numbers, to find
A geometric increase in the slow
Arithmetic click through the turnstiles of class.

Bare-headed unity, alfresco,
Differences suspended, just for a while, mind,
Among such dreams of cheering, dreams of grass.

The surge of gender's limitation's
Hard to resist when Bernie scores,
Held in too long, like self-, like crowd-control.

And weekdays the silent stand still roars
With the reproach of generations:
All we are saying is give us a goal.

21

NOTHING PERSONAL

We hate Tories
And we hate Tories
We hate Tories
And we hate Tories
We hate Tories
And we hate Tories
We hate Tories
And we hate Tories
We hate Tories
And we hate Tories
We hate Tories
And we hate Tories
We hate Tories
And we hate Tories
We hate Tories
And we hate Tories
We hate Tories
And we hate Tories
We hate Tories
And we hate Tories

We are the Tory
Haters.

PECULIAR

'Come now you rich, weep and howl for the miseries
that are coming upon you. Your riches have rotted
and your garments are moth-eaten. Your gold and
silver have rusted, and their rust will be evidence
against you and will eat your flesh like fire. You have
laid up treasure for the last days. Behold, the wages
of the labourers who mowed your fields, which you kept
back by fraud, cry out: and the cries of the harvesters
have reached the ears of the Lord of hosts. You have
lived on the earth in luxury and in pleasure; you have
fattened your hearts in a day of slaughter.'
(The Epistle of James, 5)

Peculiar how I can't resist
(And me a happy Atheist!)
This kind of stuff, the simple force
Of all that anger, still the source
Of who I am. And though it dried
Up long ago, in dreams I've tried
To trace that sandy river floor
Of prophecy and metaphor
To find its spring, a muddy pool
Of memories of Sunday School
And Chapel, dusty, mote-filled halls
With smiling shepherds on the walls.
Exactly half my life I spent
Inside some woolly shepherd's tent!
At night I'd get myself to sleep
By counting flocks of long-lost sheep
In that suburban avenue
Where I grew up, and never knew
How strange a dream it was.
                                        Quite mad!
But grim, and infinitely sad,
To ask a child to drink from dreams
Which, though they seem to spring from streams

Of justice, always turn to sand
And slip like Hope between your hands,
Like Faith. And though I can't recall
I ever read this verse at all
Back then, it's not of course the text
It seems – the usual stuff comes next
About the need for *patience*. Wow!
The Lord of Hosts required – and how –
His labourers to sit and wait
Like patient farmers for the late
And early rain to feed the roots
That give the earth Faith's precious fruit …

And so the other half I've spent
In wondering what it could have meant
Come Monday morning, looking for
Another kind of metaphor
That didn't climax with a trick
From any rich man's rhetoric,
In wondering why such vivid flowers
Of prophecy should leave wealth's power
Intact.
      Because that Good Old Cause
Was once inspired by metaphors
Like these, when English commons turned
The whole world upside down, and learned
To teach themselves to answer back,
The ancient antinomian knack
Of saying No, and took up arms
And left their little Baptist farms
To fight the seven-headed Beast,
The Church and State of king and priest
And Anti-Christ. *As if they stood*
A bloody chance! You'd think they would
Have known it, even then, that being
Right is not enough, and seeing
Kings come tumbling down's – alack –
No guarantee they won't be back.
For History never works the way

It promises, and Judgement Day
Is always just once more delayed
And God's own commonwealth's betrayed
Again. And still the rich man owns
The harvest, still the labourer groans
For justice, hungry for a share
Of labour's fruits. And everywhere
This lovely world is still in chains.

But harvesters who cry in vain
Soon learn the habit of defeat,
The tactics of a forced retreat.
Surrendering their arms except
The shield of Faith, these Baptists kept
Still bright the armour of the Lord,
Salvation's hat, the Spirit's sword.
And so they held their hope intact
And packed their saddlebags with tracts
And rode the Northern milltowns where
The Band of Saints still knelt in prayer
To Him in ugly little Zions
Built of corrugated iron,
Waiting for the day when He
Would call the Righteous to his knee
And they would take their place at His
Right hand for evermore. And this
Faint hopeless hope was all they had
To keep them going for years! Quite mad!
Though there's a logic of a kind,
If Christ died not for all mankind
But just for them, in sitting tight.
But though they kept their faith alight
This long-lost rebel regiment
Of tragicomic Old Dissent
Soon found they had a longer wait
Than even these predestinate
Old bigheads ever thought. And so
The world (like them) grew old, and lo,
This scattered army of the Saints

Grew tired and ordinary: quaint
Old codgers really: who'd have guessed
They thought that they were only blessed?
If they bore arms they hid them well
Beneath their clothes (and who could tell
They thought they were hand-picked by God
By those!)
                    It never seemed that odd
To me, at least, that Grandpa was
The way he always was, because
He looked like any gruff old bloke
Who worked for ICI and smoked
Well over twenty cigs a day
And coughed too much, who used to play
A clever game of chess and read
The *Telegraph*. Who could have said
This grumpy, stooping, kind old man
Was any other person than
The Grandpa that he seemed to be
When we would visit them for tea
Those gloomy Sunday afternoons?
The cruet that could play a tune!
The serviettes with silver rings.
Exotic salads full of things
Like radishes, and plates of spam
And luncheon meat and tongue and ham.
Brown bread and butter, tinned sardines,
And mixed tinned fruit and tangerines,
Evaporated milk, and sweets
And gingersnaps – a proper treat
For any Saint!
                    But never quite
Enough to stop the fading light,
The awkward, Sunday-evening gloom,
Descending on that neat front room.
When Grandpa went to evening prayers
The children somehow knew that there
Was something wrong, as shadows filled
That house with mystery until,

Departing, we would kiss goodbye,
Relieved to go but wondering why
Our Nana seemed so quiet and sad.

Poor Nana. Forty years she had
Endured these silent Sunday feuds
With Faith approaching sanctitude.
Her God was not so Awful He
Inspired such joyless Ministry.
She could not think that Jesus came
To save a handful known by name
Since well before old Adam's Fall.
This bunch of gruesome know-it-alls
Whose very name – Particular
And Strict (more like *Peculiar*
My father used to like to joke) –
Set them apart from other folk:
Peculiar songs, peculiar books,
Peculiar frowns, peculiar looks,
Peculiar thoughts, peculiar hymns,
Peculiar dread, peculiar sins,
Peculiar blessings. All the grief
Peculiar to his belief
That all that is not born of Faith
Is destined for eternal death,
That Duty-Faith is not enough,
And Sin's more strong than human love.
And so their love began to turn
To something else. And so they learned
Religious wars are never lost
And can't be won, and that the cost
Upon the Spirit's battlefield
Is borne by those who bear the shield
Of any Faith, who raise the banners
High of death and love.
                                    Poor Nana
Hated those peculiar books,
All those peculiar frowns and looks –
That half-baked millenarian

Tradition, half-utopian
And half the opposite. So sure
That dying was worth waiting for
They fell in love with death. Despair
Like that won't get you anywhere
Except maybe a little room
In some sad Aged Pilgrim's Home
In wintry Haydock, just this side
Of Paradise. Such lonely pride,
Among the ruins of the Fall,
To find some ground for Faith at all
When ruins were all they possessed.
And yet these Tankies of the Blessed
Liked watching all us sinners squirm
Beneath Jehovah's boot like worms,
Like dust, the vilest of the vile,
Condemned to death by necrophiles
With torturers' imaginations,
Relishing the world's damnation –
Lovely sin, indwelling sin,
That wormy one-way ticket in
The human hearts of all those who
Will perish when the lucky few
Arrive in all their glory. Gird
Their loins with truth? This silly herd
Of scared and woolly fools (the Sheep
Of Christ!) believed that they would keep
Their place booked with the Lord of Hosts
By being miserable, the most
Unhappy bunch of life-denying,
Sin-obsessed, self-justifying
Misanthropes you ever met.
Ridiculous and grim.
                              And yet,
There's other monsters worse than these,
Like those who so love life they squeeze
This lovely world to death. So long
As death legitimises wrong
And sin is just a metaphor

That justifies the rich man's law,
Their fattened hearts will always own
This lovely world, and labour groan
For all the harvests hunger's owed.

But even rigid sin's own code's
Less strict if held up to the light
Of mortal love, and every trite
Theology's a palimpsest
Where hungry, homeless, dispossessed
Desires may even now be read
Between the lines. And when they said
That she was terminally ill,
He gently nursed her dying, till
The years between them ran like sand,
Like Faith, like hope between their hands.
As useless now to fight as pray
For miracles to keep at bay
Death's wormy growth. And yet there was
A kind of miracle, because
They seemed to find a kind of first
Love at the end. And as he nursed
Her, I can't think that he believed
The woman that he loved, and grieved
For as she died, was on her way
To hell, or that love didn't pay
At last the deep, peculiar debt
Of Faith.
       And more peculiar yet,
When Grandpa died we realised
He'd never even been baptised!
This life-long Baptist-Leninist
Had somehow managed to resist
The plunge for over eighty years!
What strange theology, what fears,
What secret, ancient, nagging doubt
Was it that somehow kept him out
The water, standing at the brink
So long? I'd rather like to think

It was kind of weird dissent;
He must have known it would prevent
Him taking up his seat beside
The Lord, and that un-Sanctified,
Un-Justified, he would instead
Go straight to hell when he was dead.
Heroic stuff, to throw away
Your chance to queue-jump on the Day
Of Judgement! And for what? Quite mad
Of course, and infinitely sad,
Peculiar and pretty grim.
And yet these days I think of him
With love, respect, a kind of awe
That he, who always seemed so sure
Of everything, was clearly not,
Because he never quite forgot,
Perhaps, that old, peculiar knack
Of saying No, of holding back.

And that's a stand in retrospect
Deserves a qualified respect
From me, at least, who after all
Belonged to just another small,
Defeated, non-conformist sect
Who liked to think themselves elect
(Although, somehow, we never seemed
To win elections!), we who dreamed
A heaven on earth! What made him spurn
This fallen world's what made me turn
A Communist – to want to try
To change the world, to testify,
Bear witness to the dreaming ache
Of centuries, that day shall break
One day when Faith shall set desire
Alight and harvest-stubble fires
Burn rich men's laws, and richer fields
To hunger's rights at last shall yield.
A half-baked millenarian
Tradition! Half-utopian

And half the opposite, that paid
The difference in blood and made
The hope of centuries the price
Of building walls round Paradise.

The chiliasm of despair!
Just change the wording here and there,
And we had more in common than
I'd rather like to think or can
Explain – the same peculiar books,
Peculiar songs, peculiar looks,
Peculiar thoughts, peculiar hymns,
Peculiar dread, peculiar sins.
And him as confident there's more
To life than this, as I am sure
This life is all!
                        A regiment
Of tragicomic Old Dissent
If ever there was one! So sure
That living was worth dying for,
We lost the knack of living. Mad!
But grim, and infinitely sad,
To think that we've to do it all
Again, and face a longer haul
This time than even we had thought
Was possible, from scratch, from nought.
So we must start again to earn
The patience of despair, re-learn
The ancient antinomian art
Of saying No, and learn by heart
The tactics of a forced retreat,
Acquire the habit of defeat,
And keep alive the righteous rage
That lights the fires of every age.
And this faint, faint hope is all we've got
To keep us going. It's not a lot
I know, and yet unless the flowers
Of prophecy lay bare the power
Of wealth, unless these little, little sparks

Can fulgurate the ancient dark
And build a firmament of fire
For homeless, refugee desires
To travel by, if metaphors
Like these can't keep that Good Old Cause
Still burning bright, unless we sleep
Beneath the shield of Faith and keep
The Spirit's sword alight again
This lovely world will always hang in chains.

WAKE

Another bloody funeral,
The only time we mix
These days. And all the rancour, all
The splits since '56
And '68 – the *British Road*,
MT, 7 Days, the *Star* –
Unspoken now except in code's
Unshaken hands.
                        It's far
Too late to change all that, rewind
The tape – the Comintern,
The Khruschev Speech – to try to find
Which wrong came first, unlearn
A lifetime spent in being right
But in the wrong, and wrong
For always being right, though losing sight
Of what this meant so long
Ago's the awful price they paid
For losing all the wars
They thought they'd won, which bring us here today
To mourn that Good Old Cause.

It's cold today outside the Crem,
Enough to catch your death!
Today we should remember them
Who died, not those still left;
And yet somehow, of course, our text
Is all (between one hearse
Departing slowly and the next)
Of who is better, worse,
And who has passed away this year,
Since shivering with cold
The last time we were gathered here,
And how the world is getting old.

But when the world was young
And badly needed sorting out,
There's no-one here among
These OAPs had any doubt
It could be done, and why,
And how it needed it, and still
Were young enough to try.
They tried to change the world, until
The change they so desired
Changed them instead, and they forgot
How much the world required
Transforming, still requires a lot
More change than they had guessed.

But as for me – I came too late,
An unexpected guest
(I joined the day the USA
Invaded poor Grenada) who,
Arriving as the wake's
Just coming to an end, makes do –
As though for old times' sake –
With washing up, and stays behind
To help them clear away
A future I once thought was mine.
I want it back someday,
The history I never knew;
With half a life still yet
To live, I want their future too,
To live without regret
Who gave the only life they had
The finest cause in all
The world and watched it go to bad,
Then watched its awful fall.
The usual epitaph today's
For more than one good man.

So live that dying he can say
As these old codgers can,
And I can't, standing at the sink
Brimfull of empties, drying
Up, and trying not to think
It's over, finished, trying
Hard to breathe, to understand
The only hope I had's
Not going to work the way they planned,
Gone like this lovely world to bad.

LOCAL HISTORY

In memory of George Short

Easy then (not now!) to blame the Reds
For everything, e.g. the running fight
Outside the packed Town Hall the night
That Moseley spoke. And when the Blackshirts fled
From Doggy Market, YCLers led
The jeering crowds of shoppers. But being right
Was harder then (not now!), enough to frighten
English gentlemen who stayed a-bed
While others died, and never thought to thank
The Teesside Reds who crossed the Pyrenees
On foot, at night, in order to outflank
The marching ranks of bloody tyrannies.
Black tides they knew unchecked would burst their banks
Across the bloody Ebro to the Tees.

HARUNA MARU

For fourteen days Captain Watanabe
Enjoyed a round or two of golf, a guest
Among the sporting Teesside bourgeoisie
While T and G officials did their best
To force the dockers back. For sporting gents
In 1937 didn't mind
If Japs bought English steel for armaments.
But when he packed his irons he left behind
Five hundred tons of pig iron at the docks,
And some – now unemployed – unsporting chaps
Who'd been misled by local Bolsheviks
To play below the usual handicap
Of class and poverty: the usual cost
Of taking liberties before they're lost.

REDCAR SANDS

The red flag's flying on the front today.
It's dangerous to swim, to eat the shellfish.
To expect too much from this year's holiday.

Between the surf and the clouds from British
Steel, the last cinema holds back the tide
Of change. Here only the sand can flourish.

The walk along the blackpath from Teesside
Takes years; a sunny, Brownie dream of ease,
Of bank holidays at the good seaside,

A Republic of pleasure and release.
Tommy Chilvers lived here, died in pain,
And in between was a life on the seas,

The Trades Council, the Party, Spain.
But History never works the way its planned,
Winds blow cold and seas turn dangerous again.

The afternoon falls, the flags are furled,
And still the marram grass cuts through the sand,
Still binds the shifting dunes, this turning world.

BOLCKOWGRAD

'Middlesbrough grew and flourished like – well,
not exactly like a green bay tree: like a fungus,
should we say? Like staphylococcus in a test-tube
of chicken broth.' (Aldous Huxley)

I love this town – don't get me wrong –
This sulphurous atmosphere's
The air I breathe, where I belong.
There's something keeps me here

Among these forest chimney clouds
That spill with blood at night.
(Here's smoke enough for any proud
Would-be Stakhanovite!)

A working town that built itself,
And making money learned
The trick of turning dirt to wealth
And back to dirt, and earned

The right to set the world-wide price
With Teesside iron and steel,
A gold-rush, boom-town Paradise,
A working commonweal.

Looking back and looking down
You see the contours of this town:
        Work and money, work and money.

It's nothing to write home about,
A home itself of sorts –
But nowhere's newsboys need to shout
And home must needs be taught

That class was class and smoke was smoke
And bosses wore tall hats
When towns like this were built by folk,
A proletariat

Who built themselves, and builded here
A vision that's now gone
Whose loss still spreads like smoke, like fear,
Its calloused hands upon

This one-horse, dumb, one-party state
That put its trust in graft,
A workless town that learned too late
Hard work's poor epitaph:

Looking down and looking back
You see the shape of all we lack:
    Money and work, money and work.

TEESAURUS PARK

The morning's sharpened by the light,
The sunshine whets the sleet
That grinds the air like broken glass,
That falls like last week's snow, like shite
Among the durex in the grass
Whose iceberg field marks Spring's retreat.

Ten shillings for the suicides
Once, where this river bends,
Kept boys in work whose father's weren't,
Who fished for death on moonlit tides,
Who watched the sun come up and learned
How luck, like work and wages, ends.

This river flowed with money, men,
Reflecting skies that glowed
With work, down there, where through the trees
The Tyrant King's abroad again
Forged by the last apprentices
From something lost, for something owed.

This rubbish tip's a lesson for
The age of carnivores;
As useless while this weather lasts
To hope that work will come again, or
History unmake the past
Or rivers flow back, back to their source.

A COLD START

'Who can turn skies back and begin again?'
                    (Montagu Slater)

On the rim of a cracked, unwashed sink,
Beyond the new housing estates,
On the edge of this cold Northern town,
At the end of an unfurrowed field
Where the cows amble, aimless, to drink,
The clouds are held frozen, the weight
Of the morning is turned upside down
And History's new skies are congealed
In a thin skein of ice, this bright light.

But brightness fades soon as the mist
And the day digs as hard as the ground
Beneath this late, sudden, hard frost,
Under ice, where shines something so bright,
A Caribbean blue, amethyst
As the sky, as an island that drowned,
As the morning's new jewel is lost.

VICTORY IN EUROPE

'Everything's open and clear as after the flood,
immense chaos, but new, primeval chaos, a young
world, all barriers down, a chance, a real chance
to make socialism, to build, to create, to live...'
(Corporal Randall Swingler, Eighth Army,
Italian–Yugoslav border, 1945)

Impossible today to realise
What might have been, how then it must have seemed
Impossible to fail, as criticise
All those who woke from hot and thirsty dreams
Of sand, who tried to ride the roaring tides that rose
At last to flood the cities of the plain
In righteous rage.
        But why those waters froze,
Reflecting Winter's glacier face again
So soon; why, mirror-like, that paradise
Enchained like frost in human hearts held fast,
We also know, who, listening for the ice
To break, still hoping that the moon at last
Might thaw, again mistook for palm-fringed shores
Of peace the iceberg mountain face of war.

MY FAVOURITE MARTIAN

He stepped off a train from the wrong Cold War,
With crazy subtitles and a bad sound track,
Strapping the weight of half a world in his luggage,

Dressed for English weather like a mixed metaphor
And unpacking gifts tied, like tongues, with language.
But though he spoke in perfect syntax,

The local accents proved difficult at first:
He tried so hard to master 'unemployed' and 'duke',
Rolling his tongue round new ideas

Beyond belief, a lexicon of old English words
Comic and painful as onomatopoeias.
Lies are hard to translate, gobbledygook

For beginners, like brand-names, like Democracy.
Here every tongue's out on parole, life sentences
Of class, education, geography, precise as riddles,

Every helpful synonym another simile.
And meaning came whistling across from Mittel
Europa to fill those eager silences,

Like an international call with a two-second delay.
And then he left, and there I was, miming farewell,
Lost for words, watching the train pull out of the station,

Leaving us here so far apart, so far away,
And me so far from home, an alien,
Where everyone's pain has a different smell.

LEAVING FOR CAPE HORN

The leaping lines of sky and trees and wire
Give chase like dogs and kids and streams;
Poor England lifts her skirts and tries to run,
But London's close behind us, skies on fire,
Violent and imperial it wants her sons.
Through fields of rape a different country dreams.

Old men stoop forever in their evening gardens,
A perfect cross is never met and children climb
The slide's endless steps to heaven. The lights
Go up in the train, as dusk falls, hardens.
It's a long way off, not here, which is all right,
Like this lovely English summer evening in wartime.

Like these squaddies opposite, who must defend
A different country, quiet now, staring at the darkness.
Next year we shall be easier in our own minds perhaps,
But we all know exactly where this journey ends:
You can't stop a runaway train, and death needs no maps.
There's no return on History's express.

MISTAKEN FOR A BEGGAR WHILE READING J.B. PRIESTLEY ON KINGS CROSS STATION

It's sentimental stuff, all right,
Thumbs up, three cheers for English decency –
As well expect a cup of sweet strong tea
To quench the fires with which this country burned.
And yet, round wireless sets on Sunday nights,
All commonsense and cheerful grins.
Each week the common people gave the bird
To dreadful, corny, ENSA turns
Like Hitler, Göring, Chamberlain,
Uncommon now, but undeterred
By then by class, a People's War
Where commonsense and decency might win.
Two jaunty fingers up for evermore
To stuffed-shirts, Blimps and all the rich
Who took such great offence
At classless wartime's commonsense,
The common hopes and terrors which,
Though winning war at such expense,
Yet hardly knew what winning meant.
For victories are sooner lost
Than any wars, and common wealth is sooner spent
Than private property. And all it costs
Is common decency, is twenty pence, to learn
How hard the common beggars now must beg to earn
The price of drinking tea in England.

LIVING AND LEARNING: A STUDENT'S GUIDE

*'Universities engage in adult education not only to teach
but also to learn…'* (Edward Thompson)

Another bloody elegy, another double-cross,
For something every student ought to know:
That living is a constant debt to pay with what we learn,
And learning is the sum of what we owe.

Instead of paying History back we sell it at a loss,
To buy what we don't need with what we had,
And all I've learned is how this surge of useless anger turns
Like something decent, something good, to bad.

This selling is a dangerous game, you can't sell something twice
When work is still a marketplace for buyers;
And living's just a lesson in defeat and what it costs,
And learning that is all this world requires.

There's nothing you can buy with what you get that's worth the price,
What's gone is gone, you can't buy back the past
When everything of value, every inch of ground is lost,
And nothing's true and nothing decent lasts.

Don't let them tell you otherwise, there's nothing like a friend
Can tell you how all living turns to bollocks in the end.

YOU KNOW THE FEELING

Oh Christ, the awful sunshine's back,
Still banging at the door,
Day in, day out, year after year,
Relentless for this volunteer,
Each day comes back for more.

Thus press-ganged for a bright career,
A future that ain't mine,
Just once I'd like to disobey
And sign this working life away,
Go back to sleep, resign.

But no's not difficult to say,
It's saying yes that's hard.
Far easier to stay in bed
To bloody swing the bloody lead
Than play their bloody charades.

Get up, get out, get on instead,
And never let them guess
You wouldn't touch a fucking thing
They dangle on their fucking strings,
Their marionette success,

The prizes they think glittering.
But never once forget
There's nothing ever justifies
Self-pity's rising costs, or buys
A future back that's let.

And so I keep this anger dry,
And so the days unwind,
Unravel like this sense of loss,
A fading signature across
The wasting days, resigned.

MAHLER'S FIFTH

'You have grown lordly in remembrance too,
ancient and gentle evenings!' (Miklós Radnóti)

Flat out on the parquet floor,
Too pissed to speak, we lay in wait
For words to come, for more, for more.
We wanted more!
                            Too late
For sleep but far too soon
To wake on such a perfect night
As this, we let the moon
Through ragged curtains, clear and bright
As our ambition, felt it trace
A silver filigree upon
Our open upturned faces,
Falling like the future on
An uncut page.
                        And suddenly,
Love spoke with tongues of fire,
And everything was ours.
Our pale and luminous desire,
As tangible and numberless as stars.
Tadzio! Oh Tadzio!
Don't go, don't go…
                            How could you know
What dark and ragged skies
Would chase away the moon
Or cast tomorrow's eager strides
In shadow's stone so soon,
Or guess the future where we all
Must live would be so sad,
Or hear the silence fall,
The History we never had,
Beneath this still and moonless night
And wonder how on earth to set this future right?

DESERT ISLAND DISCS

Only those who, waking, ran down to the sand,
Now ship-shape and scrubbed by last night's gales,
Leaping through surf at low tide like castaways
Beached on a dirty little island
Littered with sea wrack, sunbathers and dead whales,
Who kept the bonfires dry for clear days
Like this – know how it felt to see a man
Swimming towards them, to feel like Caliban.

Only those who listened to the stranger's speech
While the sea looked the other way
Saw fabulous cities fall, sacked by the sand,
Who smelt diesel rumours creep up the beach,
And pitied the pity of the castaway,
Whose silence hath cheated us of this island –
Know the cost of Empire, buying and selling
Ourselves for cargo cults, which first was mine own king.

Only those who breasted the tide and could not swim
And made a religion of the sea
Knew why he spoke of water with such respect,
And how it had almost defeated him,
Embraced the nakedness of the refugee,
And watched all hope of rescue wrecked
In sight of land, the last hopeless chance for years,
Whom he taught language – know now how to curse.

And only those of us who can't say whether
This black tide will fall back at last,
If thunder still blows hoarse or continents will wait
Or if the Flood won't last for ever –
Know the ruin floating past
Is fuel for fires we must create
Again, to keep the world's one hope still burning,
Above high water. Thus may we too die learning.

AS THE OX PLOUGHS

In memory of John Miles Longden

Across the room the shadows fall
As day retreats inside,
Light dies by inches, down the wall.

This day last year you died,
A scruffy polymath, guru,
Professor, tramp and guide.

The roundest punk I ever knew,
Unlucky poet (and Red
Since Oxford back in '42 –

Far better read than dead!)
A home-grown, Boro' archimage,
A much missed, loud, big-head,

A talking bookcase, head case, sage.
Adonis dressed in black,
You never needed act your age,

John. Dionysiac
Old bugger you, still undismayed
At seventy, though racked

By all those breakdowns – Adelaide
And Lagos, Barrackpore
In 1943, which made

You lurch for evermore
Between elation and despair,
And blew to seed all your

Good looks. Behind this dreadful pair
You trod a pilgrim furrow.
Up and down you ploughed your share

Of luck and love in shallow
Soil, the only world you knew.
And though you tried to harrow

This world found it harrowed you,
Who more than fifty years
Ago left Teesside to pursue

A back-to-front career
From Addis to Witwatersrand.
Till verse forms, flowers and fears

With Latin roots in shaking hands,
The radical returned
To shake the roots of his own land.

So oxen always turn
At last to plough back up the field,
And so we have to learn

To wait till barren ground will yield
To our desire. Till then
There's nothing we can do. But we'll

Defeat them yet, John, when
The oxen turn, *boustrophedon*,
To till the world's one hope again.

And still the street lamps flicker on
Beneath this silk-moon sky.
And though the world's one hope is gone,

It's still the reason why
All art still burns a smoky prayer
To live before we die,

And stop this spinning world somewhere
Between elation and despair.

AFTER THE DELUGE

In memory of Margot Heinemann

'You who will emerge from under the flood
In which we have gone under
Remember when you speak of our failings
The dark time too which you have escaped.'
                   (Bertolt Brecht)

Margot is dead, and the sun is out,
And the wet London streets from the train
Are lovely, dazzling rivers of brass
Bursting their banks in the rain –
A submarine city, a mirage, a drought,
An ocean of sand in this hour's empty glass.

History's an iceberg, a desert of snow,
And the future's a hole in the ice,
The cities of sand are all raining down,
And glaciers float in the skies,
And swimming in sand, down we all go,
Still dreaming of water, together we drown.

Nothing is constant but change, but this weather,
But sinks to the bottom one day.
The nearest we get to the Land of Cockaygne
Is a vision of clouds, up, up and away
And over the mountains, still wheeling for ever
Like ashes and dust, still falling like rain.

STRANGE FELLOWSHIP

A Reply to Sean O'Brien's 'Never Can Say Goodbye'

'Morality… dies, when Dulness gives her Page the word.'
                                    (Alexander Pope)

Farewell then, Sean O'Brien, tara,
Adieu, goodbye and au revoir
And all the other things you say
When fellowship has had its day.
I'd really like to wish you well
(The usual way to say farewell),
To be there when the motorcade
Drives through the tickertape parade,
To see you off, to shake your hand,
Fall in behind the marching band
And join the crowds down at the quayside,
Bringing thanks from all on Teesside.
You remember us, no doubt?
It isn't much to shout about,
I know, this Ironopolis
But even here, a dump like this,
A very unimportant town
A very, very long way down
The wooded slopes of Mount Parnassus –
Even here, in evening classes,
Writers' workshops, groups, maybe
There's someone writing poetry
Who, pausing at their clumsy rhymes,
Has looked to you for help sometimes,
For inspiration, someone who
(Who knows?) would like to write like you.

I know we shouldn't be dismayed
To find our heroes' feet are made
Of clay, and yet your valediction
(More a grumpy *male*diction)

In *The Page,* your farewell to
All those who want to write like you.
Surprised a lot of folk down here
Who'd only known you these two years.
We'd barely got to know you, Sean.
So short a time to earn your scorn?
You must have broken lots of hearts
Among the desks at Northern Arts
With such plain-speaking, clever stuff.
How brave! Such risks! You must be tough.
To ridicule the amateur
In crafty tri/quatrameter:
To tell the world the truth in rhymes
Denouncing those whose only crime's
The hope that they one day might write
As well as you.
                           A noble fight!
A case of inequality
Fit subject for your poetry!
Strange Fellowship indeed to choose
The weakest people to abuse.
To use your talent to expose
The dreadful tyranny of those
Who want to write as well as you.

I'm sorry, Sean, this just won't do.
Perhaps you thought that it was funny
Calling us whose hard-earned money
Helped to pay your bills, although
You really should have let us know
Before your bags were packed to go
That you don't care for people who
Might want to write as well as you
And sooner stopped the whole charade.
Sure, writing's hard, and teaching's hard,
And teaching writing's hardest. So?
What's new? Don't say you didn't know,
Or thought this job a sinecure
To take while you were writing your

Next book, a twenty-four month rest,
Or that you never even guessed
You'd work with those who lack the right
(By virtue of their class) to write
As well as (thanks to your class) you.

I'm sorry Sean, it just won't do.
For Christ's sake, man, where's your respect?
And what the hell did you expect?
We're thick up here, not civilised,
The wonder is you're so surprised.
But since you need an explanation:
Let's think – well, class? Or education?
Three hundred years of Eng. Lit.
Where most of us don't seem to fit?
Or Gender? Opportunity?
Just think about it, Sean, could be
There's reasons why so many won't
Ever write at all, or don't
Believe that lives like theirs belong
In books. Like being told it's wrong
For even daring to have tried
By fat old gits like you in snide
And graceless verse. The wonder is
So many try despite all this,
In spite of poems by dickheads who
Want no-one else to write – like you.

But common flowers, like common rhymes,
Grow anywhere at any time:
Old-fashioned verse, the second-hand,
The second-rate, the sometimes bland,
Are not *addresses*. What's for you
Derivative can still seem new
To those who have to run so hard
To keep up with the *avant-garde*.
And what to you seems out of date
May still for others validate
Experience, language, aspiration:

All poetry's an affirmation.
Every poem somehow conveys
To someone somewhere something, says
It's *possible*, this stuff is ours,
Not just for those in Ivory Towers,
Parnassian big-heads who condemn
All those who want to write like them.

It's such an obvious argument –
I wonder if you really meant
To say the silly things you say?
Or why I feel such sharp dismay
At such a trivial poem as yours
That sneers at all us Northern bores
When there's a world of grief out there
On which to hang my own despair.
But that's the point. There's nothing much
Can help us now, though small things (such
As poetry) can still defray
The cost of anger, mute dismay,
The helpless rage, the speechlessness
That shapes my life as we progress
In ways I cannot comprehend
Towards the fucking awful end
Of such an awful century.
Small things then (even poetry)
In times like these bear heavy loads.
Like refugees they crowd the roads.
If you want reasons to despair,
There's still a world of grief out there,
A world that needs some looking after
Not the sound of poets' laughter,
Reasons why there's others too
Might need to write as well as you.

This laughter fooled me for a while –
Not Horace, surely? Not his style.
Then Swift? The toilet jokes are right,
The misanthropic touch a mite

Too strong. It's not original
Enough for Dryden: Juvenal?
This putting others in the stocks
Because they are too 'orthodox',
Then throwing dirt, and then accusing
Us of liking dirt, of choosing
To be dirty – Pope's my guess:
A *Dunciad* for Northern Arts!
But who's to play old Cibber's part?
If Dullness reigns up here alone
Which Fellow sits upon the throne?
It doesn't wash, this lonely prophet
Role of yours, O'Brien, come off it –
Poet in the wilderness
Who's writing for the Murdoch press!
Two Fellowships and three good books
Behind you give you clout – for fuck's
Sake, Sean, you don't get two years' dough
Because you swim *against* the flow.
You're home, you've made it, you're *inside*.
We looked to you to open wide
The gates of privilege, not to wall
The gardens up once and for all:
'You do not scan, keep off the grass.
Your poetry's too working-class!'
Strange sentiments from one whose job
Was not to rail against the mob
Like any anti-Jacobin
But break the gates and let us in.
A proper bloody Socialist
Who gets his knickers in a twist
When comrades come too close (or near
Enough to smell). Let's get this clear –
The great unwashed may be all right
So long as they don't try to write
As well as you!
                    Oh dear, oh dear,
I know you think we're thick up here,
But funny, as you rightly say,

How all things lead us back this way
To (whisper) ideology.
For grumpiness can also be
A form of politics, a kind
Of honourable, bad-tempered line
Of loud-mouthed, bar-stool Edmund Burkes.
Gate-keeping can't be easy work,
I know, a job for those with clout,
To lock the gates and so keep out
Us stupid, common, Northern bores
(But not one, Sean, I thought was *yours*).
The genuine patrician pose –
To wrap your arse around your nose,
And say we stink! And there you sit,
Sean, two years on, still talking shit.
An old, old trick for those with power
To look down from your Ivory Tower
And tell all those who live below
You're suffering from vertigo
Just watching us! Because we're small
We make you think you're going to fall!
Like any crusty Tory toff
You lift your snout from out the trough
To warn us that the richest food's
Too good for swinish multitudes.
But swinish multitudes make do
With what we're left by pigs like you
Who finish pissing in the trough
And then complain the swill's gone off!
You needn't worry, Sean, I'm sure
That even pigs will fly before
The biggest porker misses out!
The biggest swines don't go without
In this world, Sean. And that, I guess,
Is what I'm struggling to express:
Hard times like these mean even verse
Must choose to help or make things worse,
That even poets need to choose
If you've a talent to abuse

To bite the hand etc, or
The audience you're writing for.
And that's the least that you can do
Who writes as well as – well – as you.

Goodbye then, Sean, enjoy your trip,
And take your fucking fellowship.
I'm sorry Sean, it just won't do.
We hoped for rather more from you.
I'm sorry too for being so
Long-winded, but you ought to know
Old reds like me get really mad
To see old reds like you go bad.
Tara, adieu, fuck off, farewell,
We hope to see you back in hell –
Or Middlesbrough, as you might say!
And if you do, perhaps you'll stay
Just long enough next time to earn
Some fellow-feeling, listen, learn
Some manners, Sean. For even you
(Who knows?) could learn a thing or two
From those – you've guessed – the many who
Must always write as well as you…

BEADNELL BAY

More world shines back from this wet beach
Than I can ever know,
Love plumbs more deep than our crab lines,
Beneath the shifting sand, below
The rocks, beyond the wide sunshine,
The pool's still brim, my reach.
Far out to sea the years pull slow,

Where all is sand between the tides,
And time that sand achieves
Takes time, everything to sand.
But something tugs the line and we've
A bite; nets tumble in my hand
As pincers grip the sides,
As love pulls tight, tight, dares hardly breathe.

[handwritten margin notes: /takes /tremble]

EGERTON STREET

'I think the cause too good to have been fought for.'
(Andrew Marvell)

One more dark, wet, orange night to inhabit,
Walk down, splash through, soak up, at last admit,

One more defeat to bite on, chew on, swallow.
There's still worse to come, more rain to follow,

Like this helpless anger, this year's new dismay,
Which blows relentless, blows its strength away.

So many torrential defeats, such dark weather,
Pressing down and through the leaking leather

Of my boots, vulnerable as faith, or love.
You cannot be gloomy enough. Enough.

OBLOMOV IN LOVE

Not all the mornings in the world
Could ever warm enough
To break the lock on this iron air
That prisons every public love,
Or melt the ice beneath the snow,
Release the ground beneath the ice,
That frosts in chains the only world we know
Until the moon again begins to rise.

Not all the nights beneath the moon
Could ever freeze enough
To turn the key on freedom's cell
That unbinds every private love,
Or wipe the taste of your salt thighs,
Enclose again this maidenhead,
Till morning breaks at last with open eyes
And glaciers start to crack beneath this bed.

SHORT WALK TO FREEDOM

Mandela's free at last. And all I know
Is how it feels to lose my kids. He smiles
And waves, and walks towards the crowd, as slow
And irresistible as all the miles
Across this kitchen table's sad frontier.
The TV counts the minutes, we count the loss:
It costs so much, so many painful years
To reach that line
                      and so few steps to cross.
For once, perhaps, I wasn't always wrong,
And should be joining in, but not today.
A world away, the crowd bursts into song,
As I just watch myself just walk away,
For every history must run its course
A long way from the sound of slamming doors.

A SENSE OF PLACE

We wait in the quiet of a new house
For the old ghosts to arrive;
The wallpaper curls like mushrooms
Down hollow, haunted corridors
And windows hang like mirrors on secret lives
In empty, tragic, sunlit rooms.
At first we talk in whispers, opening doors
Like burglars; later try to shout to claim
Possession, place and property.
Until, like helpful, hatted aunts,
They all arrive with mop and pail
To dust the strange originality
Of home.
              But just imagine once,
Another move, another life ahead.
We left no forwarding address,
And drinking tea from packing cases,
Reading unfamiliar writing on the mail,
We knew at last the ghosts had fled,
The silence ours to repossess,
Unhaunted by the echoes, missing faces,
Watched the shadows all depart,
Began to fill the house with love,
Began at last to start.

HOW BLUE CAN YOU GET?

'We lived so far back in the woods, we never did
get chance to see the sun till twelve o'clock.'

I take the record from the sleeve
And hold it like a negative,
A print whose well-thumbed edges show
The marks of twenty years ago,
When growing up was still a laugh –
An awkward, grinning photograph –
When Elmore James began to sing
One sticky Summer afternoon, and everything
We didn't know, like politics and sex,
Was limned for ever by those broken, wailing bottlenecks.

And listening now, what was more true I cannot say:
Our curling, adolescent languor,
Strung out on someone else's black dismay,
Self-pity's need to make more real
The hugeness of that small-town hunger,
Or knowing straight away that this was how I'd always feel,
That this is how the world would sound,
Twelve bars of grief and beauty, spinning round and round.

NOTES

'The Paths of Righteousness' was written during the week of the attempted coup in the Soviet Union in 1991. The last line is, of course, the last line of *Paradise Lost*.

'New Times' was begun in East Berlin in Spring 1989 and finished the night the Wall came down. Artur Becker was a German Communist killed in Spain; Ernst Thaelmann was the German Communist leader murdered by the Nazis. The last two stanzas contain lines from Book XII of *Paradise Lost*.

'No Place Like Home' is spoken by Raphael Hithloday, the traveller in Thomas More's *Utopia*.

'After the Sinking of the Titanic' starts where Hans Magnus Enzensberger's *The Sinking of the Titanic* ends. The last stanza contains one and a half lines from Andrew Marvell's 'The First Anniversary of the Government Under His Highness the Lord Protector, 1655'.

'Getting Nowhere' includes a line from A.L. Morton's translation of 'The Land of Cokaygne'.

'Nowhere Special' is spoken by William Morris.

'My Favourite Martian' ends with a line from Craig Raine's 'A Martian Sends a Postcard Home'.

'Leaving for Cape Horn' borrows a couple of lines from Philip Larkin's 'Homage to a Government'.

'Desert Island Discs' uses Bertolt Brecht's *'Berichte über einen Gescheiterten'* ('Report on a Castaway'); there are also a couple of lines from *The Tempest* here.

In 'As the Ox Ploughs' the Greek word *boustrophedon* describes the turn of a team pulling a plough at the end of a field, right to left.

'Strange Fellowship' is a reply to Sean O'Brien's 'Never Can Say Goodbye', first published in *The Page* (July/August 1994 supplement to *The Northern Echo*) and subsequently collected in *Ghost Train*.